THE SONGS OF
JOHN JACOB NILES

FOR HIGH VOICE AND PIANO

D1105757

New Edition Containing
Eight Additional Songs

With a Preface by JOHN JACOB NILES

G. SCHIRMER, Inc.

DISTRIBUTED BY

HAL•LEONARD®
CORPORATION
7777 W. BLUEMOUND RD. P.O. BOX 13819 MILWAUKEE, WI 53213

Ed. 3788

Preface

What can the composer of a song collection say about his work, except that he likes it, the publisher likes it, and we both hope that you, the singers of the world, will also like it? So, since critical evaluation is out of the question, perhaps some historical background may be of interest.

This collection contains the songs which the public has taken most completely to its heart. Perhaps they are the best songs I have written. But not necessarily so. "Best" is a word easy to use but hard to define. Among them are some songs that have been ruthlessly pirated, on the erroneous assumption that anything connected with John Jacob Niles was folk music and therefore in the public domain.

There is a story told of a quack-healer operating in a remote rural area who was called in to treat a man suffering from a gigantic stomach ache. While examining his patient, he happened to glance under his bed, where he saw a great collection of lobster and shrimp shells. Concluding that his patient had overeaten of crustaceans, he based his treatment on this entirely correct conclusion, and the patient recovered. Encouraged by this success and being called in to see another patient, he again glanced under the bed, where he saw a collection of harness. "Ah-ha," he said to himself, "the man has eaten a horse." But, alas, the man had not eaten a horse, and so the treatment, based on an erroneous conclusion, missed its mark, and the patient died.

So it is with me. Because I have been a singer of traditional ballads like *Barbary Ellen, Mattie Groves,* and *The Hangman,* the half-informed have assumed that everything I sang was traditional music, whereas in fact much of it had been composed in the manner of the folk music with which I grew up and which is, even unto my eighty-fourth year, my area of operation.

The story of *I Wonder As I Wander* has been told often and in detail, which though entertaining, is not important. Suffice it to say that I wrote it in 1933, based on a fragment I overheard in the courthouse square in Murphy, N.C. *Go 'way From my Window,* the earliest of my compositions, was written in 1907-1908 for a girl with blue eyes and blond hair of whom I was greatly enamored. In the case of *Black Is The Color Of My True Love's Hair* a more detailed explanation is in order, because the text is indeed in the public domain, but the tune (which is the tune now employed wherever the song is sung) was composed by me, because I felt that the traditional one, dull beyond belief, was unworthy of that fine text.

As for the Gambling Songs, they spring from my fascination in general, and in particular, with the gamblers who operated on the Ohio River when I was a young man. I made the original sketches for these songs while on a trip to the Reel Foot Lake country with my father before World War I and I wrote them in the 1920's — all except *Gambler's Lament,* which was composed on forty-eight hours'

notice at the request of my publisher, who felt the group needed one more highly dramatic song.

Jesus, Jesus, Rest Your Head came into being because my mother and I visited a family named the Grahams, who, at the turn of the century, lived in Hardin County, Ky. My mother noted down a "little Christmas song" they sang, for I was too young at the time to take it down myself. About 1909, after I had written *Go 'way From My Window,* my mother gave me a few slips of jumbled notes and said, "Here, see if you can make a song out of this." *Jesus, Jesus, Rest Your Head* was the result.

I wrote *Carol of the Birds* for my older son, Tom, when he was four years old. *What Songs Were Sung* was written for the late Gladys Swarthout and first performed by her.

The singer will find two songs here which bear no obvious relation to folk music, except insofar as everything I write has surely been influenced by it. The earlier of these is *The Lotus Bloom,* which has a text translated from the Chinese for me by a Chinese student at the University of Cincinnati while I was studying at the Conservatory. The first sketch of this song goes back to about 1920.

The most recent song in this collection is *Evening.* The text is by the late Thomas Merton, Trappist monk, poet, and philosopher, who lived at the Abbey of Gethsemani, not many miles from my farm. It was my good fortune to know him during the latter years of his life, and this association led to the Niles-Merton Song Cycles, which consist of twenty-two songs based on poems which Merton either wrote or translated.

No more than half a dozen of the twenty-two were written before Merton's tragic death in December, 1968, but these few he did hear. He came to my studio in Clark County, Kentucky, and when he heard Jacqueline Roberts, soprano, sing them, he wept. This, as I remember, was in the late summer of 1968, just before the trip to the Far East from which he never returned.

From my earliest days, I have been writing poetry as well as music, and recently I wrote a poem which could perhaps serve as a preface to this collection. Indeed, we (I mean my publishers and I) might have omitted the preface and simply printed the poem.

When I am just a whisper in the wind,
The wind that blows so often east to west,
When I am just a whisper in the wind
And all the breath that once did raise my voice
Has joined the breath that whispers in the wind,
Even then my song will never die
And join the ghostly whisper of the wind,
Even then my song will never be
Hung on willow trees that sway with the wind,
Torn and tattered as mouldering dust.
Even then my song will swirl and spin
And find men's hearts to rest therein:
Even then my song will swirl and spin.

JOHN JACOB NILES
Kentucky (1975)

Preface to the New Edition

When John Jacob Niles wrote the preface to the 1975 edition of the songs and concluded it with the poem, "When I am just a whisper in the wind...," he was perhaps foreseeing this enlarged 1990 edition of his work. The poem ends with the lines, "...Even then my song will swirl and spin. And find men's hearts rest therein..."

John Jacob Niles's concert career ended in 1978 and he died in 1980, but the singer Jacqueline Roberts (with Nancie Field as her accompanist) appeared in many of his concerts during the last dozen years of his stage career and has continued to sing his music on the concert stages of America. Many of these performances are made up entirely of the music of John Jacob Niles. Only rarely does she make an appearance without featuring at least one of his songs.

This new enlarged publication contains all the songs in the 1975 publication, plus eight more. These eight are among the ones that Jacqueline Roberts has found most effective and which her audiences have liked best. The 1990 edition has had the benefit of her many years of experience with the Niles catalogue, and she has also been most generous of her time in reading the early proofs.

RENA NILES

Contents

Go 'way from my window

Words and Music by
John Jacob Niles
Arranged by the composer

Gently, without dragging ♩= 88

Voice

Piano

Go

'way___ from my win-dow, Go 'way___ from my door, Go
give you back your let-ters, I'll give you back your ring, But I'll
go tell all my broth-ers, Tell all my sis-ters, too, That the
on your way, be hap-py, Go on your way and rest, Re -

'way, 'way, 'way from my bed-side And both-er me no more,___ And
ne'er for-get my own true love As long as song-birds sing,___ As
rea-son why my heart is broke Is on ac-count of you,___ Is
mem-ber, dear, that you're the one I real-ly did love best,___ I

both- er me   no__ more._____   I'll
long as song - birds   sing._____   I'll
on ac- count of__ you._____   Go
real- ly did love   best._____   Go 'way__ from my win-dow, Go

'way__ from my door,   Go 'way, 'way, 'way from my bed - side   And

rit. e dim.

both- er me no more,___ And both- er me   no__ more.

The Black Dress

Text adapted and Music by
John Jacob Niles

mourn. Fa la la la la la la la la, Fa la la la la la, But

he is mis - tak - en if he thinks she will mourn. For we'll build her a

cab - in on yon moun - tain high Where the wild birds can't find her nor

hear her heart cry. Fa la la la la la la la la, Fa la la la la la

la, Where the wild birds can't find her nor hear her heart cry. Take

warn-ing, take warn-ing, young la-dies pray do, For you are quite

luck-y that this is not you. Fa la la la la la la la la, Fa la

la la la la, For you are quite luck-y that this is not you.

The Lass from the Low Countree

Text adapted by J.J.N.

Music by
John Jacob Niles

sor - row! Now she sleeps in the val - ley where the wild - flow-ers nod, And

no one knows she loved him but her - self and God. _____ One

morn, when the sun was on the mead, He passed by her door on a

milk-white steed; ____ She smil-ed and she spoke, but he paid no heed. Oh,

sor - row, sing sor - row! Now she sleeps in the val - ley where the

wild - flow - ers nod, And no one knows she loved him but her - self and God. ____

____ If you be a lass from the Low Coun-tree, Don't

8 -

love of no lord of ___ high de-gree; They hain't got a heart for sym-pa-thy. Oh, sor - row, sing sor - row! Now she sleeps in the val - ley where the wild - flow - ers nod. And no one knows she loved him but her - self and God. ___

Evening

Thomas Merton*

John Jacob Niles

Now in the mid-dle of the lim-pid__ eve-ning, The moon speaks clear-ly to the hill.__ The wheat-fields__ make their sim-ple mu-sic, Praise the qui-et sky.__ And

* From "A Man in the Divided Sea"
© 1946 by New Directions Publishing Corporation.
Used by permission of Curtis Brown, Ltd.

words _____ that flow-er On _____ lit - tle voi - ces, light as stems of lil - lies, stems of lil - lies. And

where blue heav-en's fad-ing fire last shines, _____ Re - flect-ed in the pop - lar's _

rip - ple, One lit - tle wake - ful bird, Sings like a show - er,

lit - tle wake-ful bird, Sings like a show - er, _____ like a show - er. _____

I wonder as I wander

Collected by
John Jacob Niles

Appalachian Carol*
Adapted and arranged by
John Jacob Niles

*In the version of John Jacob Niles, included in "Songs of the Hill Folk", published by G. Schirmer, Inc.

When Ma-ry birthed Je - sus, 'twas in a cow's stall, With

wise men and farm-ers and shep-herds and all. But high from God's heav-en a

star's light did fall, And the prom - ise of a - ges it then did re-call.

Black is the color of my true love's hair

Text collected and adapted by
John Jacob Niles
Music by John Jacob Niles

love ___ the grass where - on she stands.

I ___ love my ___ love and ___ well she knows, I

love ___ the grass where-on she goes; If ___ she on ___ earth no ___

more__ I __ see, My life____ will quick-ly leave me.

mp

I __ go to__Troub-le-some* to mourn, to weep, But

sat - is-fied I ne'er can sleep; I'll__ write her a note in__

a few lit-tle lines, I'll suf - fer death ten thou-sand times.

* Troublesome Creek, which empties into the Kentucky River.

The Lotus Bloom

Anonymous adaptation
from the Chinese

John Jacob Niles

When hearts are turned to fil - a - ments of sand,

What is there left?

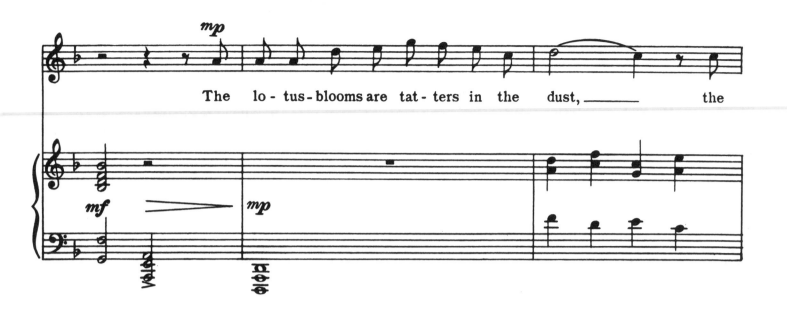

The lo-tus-blooms are tat-ters in the dust, _____ the

stream is dry, ___ the wind is sti-fled in the sum-mer's rust. Clouds shred the

sky, the lute is list-less in the troub-led hand,

the pen is cleft._____

When hearts are turned to

fil - a - ments of sand,   What____ is____ there   left,

what   is   there   left?_____

For Gladys Swarthout

The Carol of the Birds

Words and Music by
John Jacob Niles

Christ-mas day in the morn - ing, cu - roo, cu-roo, cu - roo,_____ cu-

roo, cu - roo, cu - roo._____ The lark, the dove, the red - bird came, cu-

roo, cu - roo,__ cu - roo,__ The lark, the dove, the red - bird came And

wor-shipped there in Je - sus' name, On Christ-mas day in the morn - ing, cu-

roo, cu-roo, cu - roo, _____ cu - roo, cu-roo, cu - roo. _____

The owl was there, his eyes so wide, cu - roo, cu-roo, _ cu - roo, _____ The

roo, cu - roo,____ cu - roo,____ The shep - herd knelt up - on the hay, As

an - gels sang the night a-way And God pro-claim-ed the ho - ly day, cu-

roo, cu-roo, cu - roo,_____ cu - roo, cu-roo, cu - roo.____

Sweet little boy Jesus

Words and Music by
John Jacob Niles

1. Sweet lit - tle boy Je - sus in man - ger so low,___ Sweet lit - tle boy Je - sus, we nev - er did know You were a God and a
2. No place for the Moth - er, no place for the Son,___ No place for to rest ___ the new - ly-birthed one; See how the shep - herds did

friend of ours, too,___ Sweet lit - tle boy Je - sus we nev - er knew.___
seek out a shed___ And make in the man - ger the Christ-child a bed.___

3. The ox and the sheep___ stand si - lent - ly by,___ While
4. Sweet lit - tle boy Je - sus in man - ger so low,___ Sweet

an-gels car - ol - in' did fill up the sky.___ The folk in the vil - lage slept
lit - tle boy Je - sus, we nev - er did know You were a God and a

si - lent - ly on,___ Not know-ing that this was the birth of God's Son.___
friend of ours, too,___ Sweet lit - tle boy Je - sus, we nev - er knew.___

For Thomas Michael Tolliver Niles on being five years of age

Jesus, Jesus, rest your head

Adapted from the singing
of three people in Hardin County, Kentucky

Adapted by John Jacob Niles

Je - sus, Je - sus, rest your head, You has got a man - ger bed.

All the e - vil folk on earth Sleep in feath - ers at their birth.

Je - sus, Je - sus, rest your head, You has got a man - ger bed.

What Songs Were Sung

Words and Music by
John Jacob Niles

stood hard by While heav'n-ly sound filled up the sky.

Now let us stand, un-cov-ered all, Be - fore this crèche in ___

low-ly stall, Where kings and an - gels dig - ni - fy God's_ gift, His Son, in hu -

mil - i - ty. We do not know, we can-not tell What

44

The Rovin' Gambler

Collected and adapted by
John Jacob Niles

Reelfoot Lake, the background for several of these "Gambling Songs", lies mostly in Tennessee (its northern tip being in Kentucky) and is one of the world's best fishing grounds. Formed by an earthquake in 1811, the lake is surrounded by country abounding in characters who seem to have walked out of the pages of folklore. According to local legend the earthquake was caused by the steamboat "New Orleans" when it made the first steam-powered journey down the nearby Mississippi River.

She pick-ed up her sat - chel And she did leave her home,___ And on the steam-er "Morn-ing_ Star" The_ two of them did roam,___ The two of them did roam, With a click clack oh and a high john-ny ho, The two of them did roam.

The Gambler's Lament

Words and Music by
John Jacob Niles

dark and the wet and the chill That comes of be - in' hanged so high On the

A little lighter in mood ♩ = 120

top — of Hang-in' Hill. When I was a young man Be - fore I was

rit....

mf

hold back

grey, — I played a man-y a card game And bet my wealth a -

way._____ But now I'm an old man And gam - blin' still_ With

hang - in' in the morn - ing On Hang-in' Hill._____ Oh they'll

rit.

As at first

hang me, they'll hang me, And I'll be dead and gone. I____

mp sombre

For Gladys Swarthout

The Gambler's Wife
(By - Low)

Words and Music by
John Jacob Niles

*colloquialism: "rather" (preferences)

Gambler, don't you lose your place

Words and Music by
John Jacob Niles

gam-bler, don't you lose your place at God's right hand

'Cause hell ain't no place for Reel-foot folk to be.

With emphasis ♩ = 132

Gam-bler, gam-bler, you is a man Think he could win ___ on ___

ev-'ry hand, But when you a die, you know right well You go-in' to go right

Gambler's Song of the Big Sandy River

Words and Music by
John Jacob Niles

My lover is a farmer lad

Words and Music by
John Jacob Niles

My lov-er is a farm-er lad who comes to me at

twi - light. _____ Mean - while my oth - er suit - ors

woo me while it is yet day - light. _____ A

butch - cher's boy, a cav - a - lier, and

one of his Maj - es - ty's most mag - ni - fi - cent _____ dra - goons.

But my lov-er is a farm-er lad who comes to me at twi-light. _____ Mean-while my oth-er suit-ors woo me while it is yet day-light. _____ The keep-er of a pub-lic house, a com-mis-si-on-aire and

one of his Maj- es -ty's most mag - ni - fi - cent _____ dra -

goons. _____ My farm- er lad loves his farm-ing and he

loves the ris -ing moon, And he cun-ning -ly watch- es my gar -den gate___ for that

pom -pous, proud dra -goon. Oh my lov - er has nei -ther cit - y clothes__ nor a

comb for his tous - led hair, But his hand - some hands are strong and brown, __ and his

rit. *a tempo (legato)*

man - ner is deb - o - naire. __ My lov - er is a farm - er lad who comes to me at

twi - light. _____ Mean - while my oth - er suit - ors

woo me while it is yet day - light. _____ A

butch - er's boy, a cav - a - lier, and

one of his Maj-es-ty's most mag-ni-fi-cent _____ dra - goons. _____

_____ But my lov-er is a farm-er lad who comes to me at

twi - light. _____

pp

pp *rapidly*

This page left blank to accommodate page turns.

The Wild Rider

Words and Music by
John Jacob Niles

bri - dle and pulls up the girth And he's off in a flash the best rid - er on

earth. He snaps on a bri - dle and pulls up the girth And he's off in a

flash the best rid - er on earth. _____ The first time I saw him was

ear - ly one spring. He was rid - ing a bron - co a high - head - ed

mong them a ring. The re-turn that I made was a far great-er thing. 'Twas a

young maid-en's heart I will have you to know,_ He had won it by rid-ing his

buck-ing bron-co. 'Twas a young maid-en's heart I will have you to know, He had

won it by rid-ing his buck-ing bron-co. Now, come all ye

Ribbon Bow

Words and Music by
J. J. Niles

think me fair.____

rit.

a tempo

a tempo

If I was like the cit- y brung and

fair with smart,_____ Ne'er a lad in

all them parts would know my heart.____

Then I'de live in Frank-fort Where all the law-in' goes. I'd lark a-bout the set-tle-ments And

wear them furr-in' clothes. If I was like the cit-y brung and

fair with smart,_____ Ne'er a lad in all them parts would

know my heart._____

Little Black Star

Words and Music by
John Jacob Niles

far. Goin' tell my Je - sus a - bout my lit - tle black

star. Goin' tell my Je - sus just where he

are. Goin' tell my Je - sus all a - bout my

star. Down in that swamp those mean old al - li - ga - tors

fight. _____ They fight all day, _____ they fight all

night. _____ Goin' tell my Je - sus how those 'ga - tors

fight. _____ Now don't you wor - ry, _____ my lit - tle hon - ey black_

star. _____ No 'ga - tor goin' to get my _____ lit - tle black

star. _____ When I get to heav-en, _____ thank Je-sus for my lit-tle

star. _____ 'Cause he's just like his dad-die _____ way yon-der

far. _____ He's just like his dad-die _____ way yon-der

far. _____

The Robin and the Thorn

Words and Music by
John Jacob Niles

poco ad lib.

dy - ing _ Sav - iour's _ head. The blood from out our Sav - iour's brow was

splashed up - on his feath - ers, And now the Rob - in's red re - sists All

poco ad lib.

wa - ters _ and _ all _ weath - ers. Would ye _ not have plucked _ that _ thorn

As that lit - tle bird did fly - ing? Would ye _ not have healed _ the _ head of

Unused I am to lovers

Words and Music by
J. J. Niles

not un-moved my song of _____ love's _____ un-sung.

Spring she brings her green and sum - mer ___ soon will shine.

Will I in this sea-son have a lov - er ___ to call _____ all

mine? For I shall bid all hap - pi - ness a -

dieu _____ Un - less some lov - er comes and gent - ly

makes my dreams come true. _____ Un - used I am to

lov - ers, I _____ am __ ver - y young. Tho' my heart is

not un - moved, my song of _____ love's _____ un - sung.

Slower

a tempo

a tempo

* *rit.*

rit.

* See page 1 for variant.

When I get up into Heaven

Words and Music by
John Jacob Niles

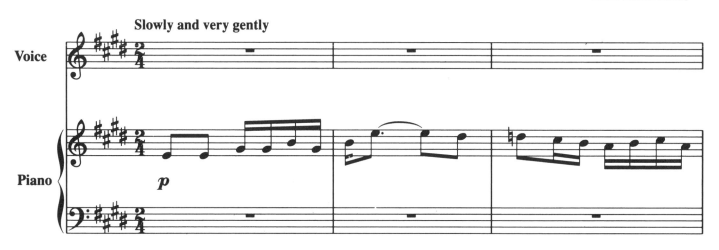

too, _____ I want you to be there too.

1. I want to see my dear old pappy
   I want to see my mama too.
   But heaven simply wouldn't be heaven
   If I couldn't be in heaven with you.

2. I know this place what they call heaven
   Is a poweful fine place for to be.
   But if you can't be with me in heaven
   It wouldn't be no place for me.

3. The Bible it tells all about heaven,
   It's a place with a wide golden street,
   But I wouldn't want to be in heaven
   If I couldn't be with you, my little sweet.

   (repeat the first verse)

The Flower of Jesse

Words and Music by
John Jacob Niles

♩ = 72 **Flowing and with great tenderness**

Voice: *mp*
There__ is a flower sprung of a tree, the root there - of is
called Jes - se. 'Tis in - deed a flow'r of Pre-cious Price for __

there is none such in all of Par - a - dise.

This is the flow'r sprung of a tree, the root there - of is

called Jes - se. It is fresh and

fair of hue, it nev - er fad - eth

rit. *a tempo*

but is ___ ev - er new. ___ This ___ is a flow - er sprung

rit. *a tempo*

of a tree, the root there - of is

called Jes - se.

There ___ is a flow'r sprung

of a tree, the root there - of is called Jes - se, the seed there - of, the seed was God's com-mand _____ sown __ it __ was by his own __ hand. _____ And __ did __ bloom this